# *Contents*

This book dedicated to women everywhere
in the world who are suffering inequality,
abuse, sexism or violence in their world.
For those who suffer in silence.

# *Illustrations*

Sebastien Meyrignac

Instagram @blackliquidink


David Van Gough

Instagram @davidvangough

davidgoughart.com/bigcartel.com


Slavae1

Instagram   @slavcom

Liv Kristin Haakerud

Instagram   @hakerud73_ed


Vanessa Weinswasser

Instagram @kunstfabrikstudio

www.behancenet/vanessa207a

Welder Wings

Instagram @welderwings

www.redbubble.com


Bijiana Milić

Instagram @biljana5095._83


Yukiphotography

Instagram @yuki.t_photography


Kirsten Schaap

Instagram @kirsketchbook

Linktr.ee/kirsketchbook

# *Introduction*

I was recovering from chronic fatigue, the unexpected nightmare that followed my cancer treatment. I think it was my body responding to all the stress I had been under for years, finally shouting for me to take notice and stop. The muscle weakness, the bouts of sadness, frustration and depression that followed were accompanied by the pandemic. In retrospect, I can see the positive side. The world slowed with lockdown and it gave me time to rest. I could start the long journey to improve my physical and mental wellbeing.
It is a year later that I am writing this, having taken up counselling and yoga to try beat the exhaustion that tried to overcome me. The fatigue was much worse than anything else I have ever experienced. I used to be very active beforehand. The saying, "You never know what's happening behind closed doors," rang true. I was often completely immobilised. Days in bed with absolutely no energy... Devastated that my body couldn't even do the simplest tasks. Only my family really knows how bad it got. If I felt well enough to go for a small walk the consequences were unbearable. I tried to push myself but even the smallest

exertion could result in the weight of the fatigue overwhelming me completely. It was an invisible struggle.

This was a significant challenge in my life but how could it be more significant than me? The truth is it wasn't, there were many more difficult times ahead. I had made the first step writing poetry now I embraced the counselling journey alongside yoga meditation and acceptance that I could only do what I could each day . The rate of recovery after a year of muscle weakness is so slow, something I found hard to cope with, but I was determined. I also wanted to show my children that sticking at something seeing it through till the end, being resilient no matter how long it took was important, little did I know there were to be several beginnings and even more endings before I would discover my scared truth and inner peace.

One year exactly since I started on the yoga mat crying with the effort it took I still lay on my mat every day and did the online class by Adriene Mishler feeling no judgement just encouragement. It was amazing how connected I felt to her gentle spirit another factor in my recovery. Just showing up some days was enough. I had practiced yoga a few times over the years.

It was such a challenge to keep motivated as my body just wouldn't do what it should. However I kept on the journey and finally a year later I am so grateful to be able to go for a walk and be ok. Yes, I still need more rest than usual but I have found a balance that works for me. I don't beat myself up if I have to go to bed for a rest during the day. I am just so grateful to be able to live a more normal full life now.

"All the world is full of suffering. It is also full of overcoming" Helen Keller

Do I see the world as others do? I am forever imprisoned in restless thoughts, yawning beneath the surface. My imagination is free but I often grieved for the things I felt were missing in my life. Of course, everyone's perception of the same thing can be different but also their response, reactions and emotional fallout is unique. Therefore in order for me to explore what had been happening to me, I had to dig deep within me to find the strength to continue. Perhaps my greatest regret is hiding so much of the difficulties I was having but my writing was always there to carry me along, to lift me to a level where I could see over the mountain I had to climb. It all started with a poem, that pivotal moment when you write something and it changes you completely. I called it "A Thirst for Me". There is no hiding from the truth of your existence. It came from my subconscious but the more I read it the more I wanted to crawl into those words and to give them more vibrancy, love and care. I wanted to give myself more love and care. A lot of my poems in the first section of this book are dark and filled with hidden meanings but they have allowed me to absorb the pages as if wrapped in a shroud of support and understanding. It was a moment of deep intimacy with myself, a feeling that I had touched on something of value and importance and that would bring me into new experiences that I could embrace no matter how vulnerable I felt. I wanted to have them in one, collection as a testament to my hard work, growth and self-acceptance.

Every human deserves to feel connected to themselves and their experiences.

We cannot invite healthy relationships into our lives without a proper sense of who we are, creating healthy boundaries and allowing time for self-love and attention without feeling guilty about it. The most important thing I have learned on this journey is of course there are days where it all becomes too much but with perseverance and reaching for support your life can change. I have passed this on to my children and hope they will carry it with them always.

I am a poet, a women who gets lost in her imagination in order to find the person she wants to be. A woman who travelled under the guise of a forgotten entity, now stepping into the heart of her emotion to become her authentic self.

I am a women longing to be me, to feel a real connection with the world and the people surrounding me.

Throughout my past, I silently went about my day quite disconnected and detached. It was a coping mechanism I had fallen into a long time ago in order to avoid my emotions. I wanted to change how I was feeling.

It is not right to pretend I didn't exist before I knew my name. I closed doors and fitted them with locks that even I couldn't disarm. I could not heal myself until I went back into those rooms that had remained dusty and unkempt, filled with memories, filled with me. There were many things in my past and present that needed healing.

Discovering a connection with your younger self truly is a gift that I am blessed to have experienced. I have been very happy in my life don't get me wrong but it is liberating to finally feel the weight of my past dissolve into the atmosphere and float to another dimension.

I would like to thank all my followers on Instagram as they have also been there with me throughout my journey supportive and encouraging. To all the people out there who need to come to a place of self-love and healing, be gentle, it doesn't happen overnight but it's definitely worth the trip.

Much gratitude to my counsellor Mary who has guided me in the process and always encouraged me to keep striving but also making me realise I deserve happiness I deserve love and most of all I deserve the freedom to do ME. Thank you to my family and friends who have supported me throughout my journey.

This is my second solo collection. If you can take something positive from my journey and perhaps delve into your inner self in the process, I will feel I have given a little back. The beginning of the end is something I understand now as every ending needs a new beginning.

Thank you to the artists who have inspired many poems and especially to those who are featured in this book.

Instagram @sineadmcgpoetry
Artwork @sineadmcgphoto
Facebook @sineadmcgpoetry
Twitter @smcgpoetry

The souls of people, on their way to Earth-life, pass through a room full of lights; each takes a taper - often only a spark - to guide it in the dim country of this world. But some souls, by rare fortune, are detained longer - have time to grasp a handful of tapers, which they weave into a torch. These are the torch-bearers of humanity - its poets, seers and saints, who lead and lift the race out of darkness, toward the light. They are the law-givers and saviours', the light-bringers, way-showers and truth-tellers, and without them, humanity would lose its way in the dark.

*Plato*

*This Book is Closure.*

*Blackliquidink*

# A THIRST FOR ME

I can't stop wanting you.
I don't know you. But you exist.

Watching me while I sleep,
Lifting me to new levels.
I am wandering through dreams
Filled with lost memories.
Shadows tracing lines on my skin.
Searching deeper for a point to begin.

I can't stop wanting to taste your lips.
To remember your shadow smile.
To gaze into your eyes in bliss.
To touch the dark thoughts within.
My tongue forms a new language.
I don't know you.
But you exist.

You have no beginning or end.
You paint colourful designs
Shaping imagination into fine art.
Artistic endeavours reflecting a
Voyage of discovery.
Spiralling forms for an eternity.
I exist.

I drenched myself in assumptions,
Now I drink in holding my breath.
A deep sip of unbearable teasing,
Pouring me engaged into reality.
I paint my distracted thoughts.
Engrave tattoos on my skin.
Absorbing ink, absorbing blood.
A thirst for creating, a thirst to heal.
I finally feel the weight of my words.
I feel the essence of me.

I can't stop wanting me.
I exist.

## *THE AFTERMATH*

I am the aftermath of a catastrophe.
The intersection of life and death.
Taking flight in solitude and harmony,
I am the singing songs of neglect.

I am the shattered illusions of past horrors,
tarred and feathered by grumbling clouds.
Imprisoned in skies of reality,
I am the suffering edges of a shroud.

I am wrapped around pain and sorrow,
Held by sleeping claws in the cold earth.
I am the lifeless wings of past pain,
Clinging to dreams of tomorrow's reign.

I am the flying dreams of sharp beaks,
Cutting into graves of rebirth.
I am a new dream of freedom.
I am the aftermath.

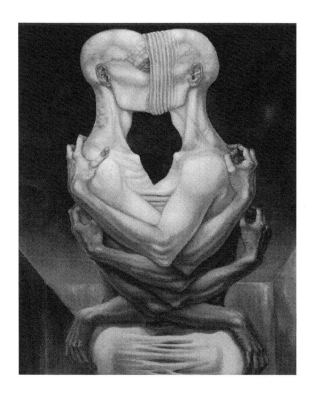

*David Van Gough*

# *CONTROL*

You extracted my ribs to make your
Arms into a cage so I couldn't escape.
Your bony fingers bored into me,
I couldn't feel me anymore.
You crushed me with your weight,
Pressing my flesh until it blackened.

You suffocated my creativity,
Blinding my vision, folding my eyes.
They blinked in the back of my head.
You swallowed my lips to silence me.

You extracted the love from my heart.
Absorbed my blood like a scavenger,
All I tasted was blurred delusions.
You tried to engulf my fighting spirit.
You wanted to exist through me for power.

I remained silent.
Uncaged in waters of illumination.
Fearless in mystical lands of darkness,
I am waiting to be embraced by the
Shadows of death.
Laid out in dusted roses.
Waiting for my last breath.

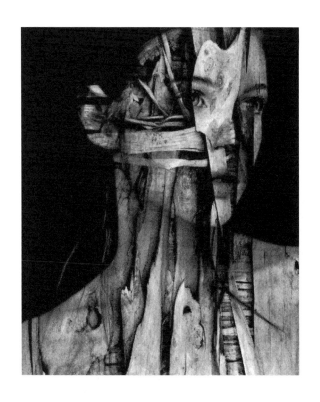

*Slave1*

## *THE EDGE OF COLOUR*

In his hands she decayed,
Unloved blossoms fell into troubled eyes.
She cannot see for she is blind.
Lost in unfathomable darkness,
The sun no longer shines.
Stricken, there is no beginning or end.
Stems explore her throat, love exhales.
Emptied there is no reality contained in a
Body, strangled and cursed.
She is buried alive, on the edge of colour.

*Yuki.t_photography*

# THE SENSES

I have no words but I have colours.
A painted body embedded in the earth.
I exist in nature only visible under the
Northern lights.
I have no eyes, but I see
Images of darkness surrounding me.

I have no ears, but I hear the call of the
Wind. A musical of intensity, caught in
Stormy weather. I have no fingers
To claw through the soil, yet
I touch you every day.
My skin lives under the skies
Pouring cold into a still heart.
I am here but I am not there.
I cradle myself with delicate care.
I am who I am, I am just me.
Floating drifting forever free.

When I meet you I stretch out my hand
Finally invite you to step forward and see
Look at your reflection,
Look at me.
Our hands meet across the waters.
Drowning in the love of our truth until
The tides carry me to you.

*Slave1*

# ECHOES OF YESTERDAY

Darkness brought me here.
A body marked by the devil,
Satanic rituals performed
Embedded with deep scathing scars.

How the imprint of the blinded past,
Drums the echoes of yesterday.
A world filled with remorse.
A body strangled by regrets.

Darkness worshipped my heart,
Filled it with an endless hunger.
You felt it pulsing, creating mayhem.
Contesting the gods of the underworld.
.
Stars aligned edged with me.
Fighting for my beloved and me.
Swirling mists swallow the
Silence of infinity.

# *THE STIGMATA*

Deep in the heart of haunting nights,
My aching limbs upon a cross.
Lashes of tears sacrificed my dreams.
Betrayed our love into unspeaking mouths.

I am a wound weeping in denial.
I am the stigmata engraved in rage.
My soul lifts to the overhanging sky.
My bleeding heart blinds your eyes.

Your kisses upon the cross of grief,
Whisper farewell to the beauty of love.
Arms pinned straining to touch your face.
My flesh cast into death's embrace.

Deep in the darkness of your dreams,
I am bared in the pearls of your eyes.
I am the heat your memories cast.
My thoughts fill your fevered night.

Oh muse of mine, held in Charon's grip,
Bite the coin, unbind your eyes.
I will call for you from beyond the grave.
I am the sovereign of humanity saved.
I am shards of light in Hades dark,
Embodied love as death embarks.

# *MEDUSA*

You were death, cold and silent.
A staring Medusa.
A heart of stone.
Kissing my eyes.  (Blinded)

You were death, roaring loudly.
An aegis shield.
A clouded mind.
Drowning my breath.  (Suffocated)

You were death, insightful and hissing.
A fire to the deities.
A flame of humanity,
Branding my flesh.   (Burning)

You were death, invisible and crying.
A passage to hades.
A helmet of thoughts.
Bleeding my veins.   (Dying)

You were death, a journeying breeze
A sleeping dawn.
A keeper of winds.
Devouring my body.   (Passing)

I am dust scattered through air,
Lamenting my soul.
Falling into your aching arms.  (Dreaming)

*Welder Wings*

# *A THIRST FOR TRUTH*

Expose the way we are through poetry.
Elevated ideas marked upon flesh.
Crucified at the border of humanity.
Yearn for more.

Yearn for something with deep foundations.
Listen to echoes of the past.
What words were spoken before the cross?
The crying, fierce and desolate.

The horizon waiting for enlightenment.
Burning in creative prose.
Bare the breast at the dawning of the day.
Yearn for more.

I hide my tears in the translucent rain.
They dance from my face like confetti.
Bare the breast to see the heart of humanity.
Expose your truth through poetry.

Yearn for more.

*Liv Kristin Haakerud*

# THE SINS OF YESTERDAY

The sins of the past, thirst her decay.
Endless torture reaching
Towards deliverance one day.
Countless lashes soaking her skin.
Flesh oozing through wounds,
Held together with pins.

She honours her dreams with
Withering stems. Engulfed by their hold,
She bleeds into them.
Creeping further into her mind,
Suffocated by thorns, blooms break and die.

Their wrath, oppressive, restraining her
Hands. Digging to honour her darkness,
Deep rooted demands.
The seeds of tomorrow break free in the
Wind, scattering the pain erasing her sins.

.

## COLLECTOR OF SOULS

You were restless, to climb into
The valley of corpses, from
The moment you sprang from the womb.
A collector of souls, hungry for the vale.
Longing to be pressed beneath
Cemented slabs and cobblestones.

You were destined to be a fugitive of
Life, rooted in darkness.
Hands with purpose, waiting
To ease the pain of death.
Digging deep into hanging veins,
Bleeding out into the earth's core.
You breathe out all life,
Inhaling oblivion.

## *MY EPITAPH*

What am I without a poem?
An unearthed body,
Digging deep into the earth.
The soil filled with monologues
Runs through my fingers.
Breaking the crusted earth into
An epiphany of ideas.
Beating my hands with stones,
A cacophony of sounds.
A heart waiting for you to
Kneel at my graveside.
A heart waiting for you to
Read my epitaph.
An epitaph smothered by dust.

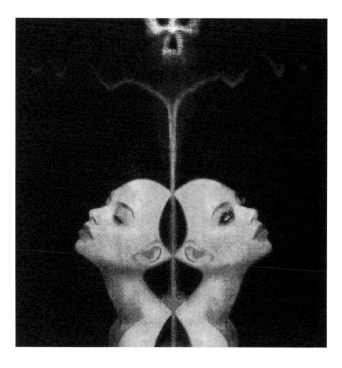

*Vanessa Wenwieser*

# THE GATE OF HORNS

She carried her dead heart
Towards the gate of horns
Dressed in black silk, breasts bare.
Eyes shut, lips smeared burgundy.
Not knowing herself,
Wisdom fell unworthy.

Wounds fostered fear in an ebony heart.
Trust broken by her eternal fear.
She gazed in wonder at the ivory gates.
A reflection of her, a reflection of dreams.
Eyes golden in contrast to the night,
Separated from the morning dawn.

She wandered through graves,
Calling her name. A loud
Applause inviting her in.
Cracking bones in clustered mouths.
Crunching teeth grinding all traces of truth.
Wisdom fell unworthy.

She sacrificed herself at the gates of hell.
Her heart bleeds eternally,
She will never tell holding herself and
Her truth in the fires of hell.
She carried her herself,
The heavy weight of the past.
Wisdom fell unworthy.

# A THIRST FOR WORDS

I never needed you, I only needed me.
My heart open longing for your love,
Only needed to become aware.
I had everything inside me.
My inner strength, my passion and
My authentic self.
My love for me cradled by the stars until
I could see the beauty beaming inside me.
I feel peace and serenity.
I feel calm in my dark depths.
Waves of past intentions, blinded by fears,
Absorbed by my poetry.
Words aflame, an extension of my reality.
I am free, the essence of harmony.
A floating shadow of alchemy.

# LOST IN MY ART

I dream of art and poetry.
A celestial palace, filled with
Dreams of eternal moons.
Filled with chambers of silver rings.
Circling naked limbs.
I dream of crystals of creativity
Sparking ideas and poetry.

Come with me into
The land of magical verses,
Away from agony.
Kiss these lips, singing spells.
Wishing for a better tomorrow.

*Welder Wings*

# A THIRST FOR BLOOD

Surrender into my bones.
Drink my blood,
Seeping into your mouth.
Spilling down your gasping throat,
Whispering words melting hearts.
Finger my secrets with your
Longing touch, rigid precision
Vibrating ownership into my body.
(I belong to you)

Submit to hunger without restraint.
Words of blood humming into lips.
 (Explore me)

Caressing sighs moaning devotion
In your name.

How can we endure?
What binds colour to your heart?

Drink my blood,
Surrender into my bones.

*Liv Kristin Haakerud*

# BOAT OF DREAMS

Take me on your boat of dreams.
Let me sleep in your eyes.
Let me be enchanted by your vision,
The way you see the world.
Let me lie beside you.
Let me watch you as you stare at the skies.
Blues colliding, reflecting our eyes.
Let me dive into the ocean, holding hands.
Surround me in your presence.
Reach for me now, floating high.
Take me to the mountain of sighs.
Let's breathe in the crisp air.
Let the mountain dew wet my lips.
As you paint the beaming beauty
The golden sun shines on the bridge of
Locks, where the river calls our name.
The ocean plays music into my heart,
Mozart waltzes ring through the air.
We travel towards mysterious places,
Dreaming of love and romance.
Take me into your heart of dreams
Let me sleep in your eyes of chance,
Until you awaken.
Until you see the colour of me.

*Biljana Milić*

# A THIRST FOR SIGHT

Absorbed by the earth,
I dream outside myself.
I am a lucid flow of air,
Rising towards the sun.
Flowering symbols of life,
stretching through darkness.

I am flesh and bone,
Held by the nature of the divine.
Held on the brink of shadows.
I am shining through the universe in death.
Gazing on the earth, watched by the moon.
I finally see the universe is on my side.

I finally am free.

Rediscovering me.

*Yuki.t_photography*

## BENEATH THE STILL WATERS

She appeared as an apparition,
Beneath the surface.
Still waters casting thoughts of utopia.
She, the light of summer,
Waiting for you to find her.

She becomes an angel of the sea.
A visionary for saints and warriors.
Breaking death into cold delight.
Strewn on the chilly ocean floor.

She moaned to the night,
Waiting to awaken, crying her lament.
Crying for your otherworldly love.

Her face a distraction, so
Pale under shady trees.
Overflowing thoughts swaying,
Through the clinging green.
Reaching for the birthplace of intellect.
An inkwell filled year after year.

*Blackliquidink*

# A THIRST FOR POETRY

Taste the language in my mouth,
Savour the poems upon your tongue.
Find love in this decaying world.
Swallow the air of translated breaths.

The beauty of space can never die.
Love is the blanket we need to survive.
The mourning of those lost moments from
Another time, float away and dissipate.

We meet in vibrant blossoming splendour,
You and I. Words flowering flourish,
Flushed into each other's devotion.
Spellbinding words, the creation of love.

The beauty of amour flowering through
Poetry. We meet where the ocean
Runs into the sky.

*I raise up my voice—not so that I can shout, but so that those without a voice can be heard. ... We cannot all succeed when half of us are held back.*
*Malala Yousafzai*

**Vanessa Wenwieser**

*Vanessa Wenwieser*

## *THE WITCHES THEY COULDN'T BURN*

The Goddess of Womanhood,
Danced in the flames.
The daughters of triumph
Rise unshackled from pain.

Woman who live, in burning
Embers of judgement.
Lament in billowing breaths,
Sighing memories of atonement.

She is the bright spark in every flame.
Rising from the ashes to
Fight against the pain.
She is no longer a spectator to
Blame and lies.
Held behind shuttered windows,
A woman denied.

She has a right to knowledge,
Blinking eyes of endeavour.
She joins her sisterhood in arms against
control forever.
She is the thunder that roars against
Prejudice and fear, pouring fire on
Discrimination, violence and tears.

She is a human, a person,
A woman of rights.
The future of us,
Holding your hands in the light.

She is a woman in freefall,                    1
Breaking through barriers of grief.
Fighting to end restrictions, held in
Traditions and false beliefs.

There are crimes against women we cannot
Tolerate or allow, laws written to exclude,
A womanhood destroyed.

The goddess of womanhood,
Danced in the flames.
Her ancestors ignite feminine energy today.
The witches you couldn't burn lit the
Torch for your path.
Raising your voices, inciting flames to flash.
She is a woman equal in any storm,
Shinning brilliantly for all the unborn.

She is a woman "Unbound and Unique "

## *FREEDOM OF REMBERANCE*

Remember me, as you gaze at the earth.
Tinged red humus, oozing acidity.
Heinous crimes, filling the soil,
Piled with torment and cruelty.
Spreading stories of torture.

I am hidden beneath this cloak of devotion.
Slowly unwinding threads of society.
I unleash all that governs me,
To stain the earth with colours of integrity.

What does the future hold?
The voiceless whispering
Stories of uncertainty into the clay.
Remember me. Stories of mortality.
Remember me.
Freedom.

*Kirsten Schaap*

# *IMBOLIC*

She shreds her flesh to offer it to the moon.
She offers peace as darkness leaves spring,
Scattering magic seeds for the festival of the
Imbolc.

She, no longer a slave to the underworld,
Stretches through the earth,
Giving women fertility in a promised land.

She holds charms of the divine.
Glittering gold into their wombs.

Holy wells fill dead eyes with unrest,
Running into the streams of her Celtic lands.
Dazzled by the moon she weaves
Freedom into the heart of every woman.

She is a goddess of grace and beauty.
She is a goddess of poetry.

She is The Imbolic.

*Vanessa Wenwieser*

# *FOREVER FREE*

You want me to stay hidden from the world.
The world to appear in glints of grey.
I carry these flowers laden in glorious seeds,
Free floating hands filled with
Miracle dreams.

Not bound or rooted in earthly endurance
Open palms serving serenity and peace.
You want me to stay hidden behind
These four walls, waiting trembling,
Clawing against the grey of the night.

I, digging my fingers searching for stems.
To stay visible free absorbing delights.
Not bound to terror of despicable nights,
Hiding under a cloak of shattered lives and
Eternal fights.

I pray that my religion embraces and
Blooms. I pray that it is not spitting,
Mourning the woman in me.
I pray that my religion illuminates all, not
Burying my heart with unwritten laws.

I scatter petals of truth for all woman to see.
The flourishing beauty in our time of need.
I sew mouths together burning in hate.
To stop angry judgements,
Whispering disgrace.

I pour flowers of peace, calming the hate
Folding petals on war torn tongues.
Soothing mouths suffocated by conflict,
Creating peace from sharp cutting stones
I hold garnets outstretched to guide our way.
No more wails or screams
Consuming our days.

I scatter petals of colour,
Weave strings into smiles.
No longer isolated in fear
Behind a veil of lies.
I am a woman born to be free
Sewing wounds of strife for the unseen.

I am a woman who speaks out
For the voiceless who grieve.
I am a woman fighting back.

I am a woman born to be free.

## THE EYE OF RA

The lion shakes his golden mane,
Roaring towards the morning star.

The yellow sun births sculptures of fire
From the womb of solar, life beings.

Sekhmet the Eye of Ra
Lifts her powerful gaze.

Her tears orbit in crosses of Ankh,
Shining symbols of eternal life.

Flooding energy and clarity into the
Mortal beings of the earth.

The right eye of the sky,
Shaping the divine female.

An undying faith,
The duality of tears.
Casting mystery in the air.

# THE LOST SOULS OF TUAM

As the sky poured down its crimson pain,
Women condemned held in holy wrath.
Blood washed the passion from their veins,
Silent prayers whispered at their graves.

Unmarked and hidden from the world.
Lost souls sang hymns, the Holy Grail.
Mothers in pain held defeated lives.
Scrubbing sins into laundry mats.

Oh righteous pleas, their stolen lives.
Babies torn apart from their mother's arms.
Hot tears stream death's cold embrace,
Babies never to be part of the human race.

Bitter tongues chant prayers to
Religious hand that cradled flesh.
Sins hidden under righteous cloaks,
Illegitimate secrets hidden, buried unrest.

With nobody to bless,
The lost souls of Tuam.
With nobody to save,
The lost souls of Tuam.
With nobody to find justice,
For the lost souls of Tuam.

As the years passed, their grief and
Suffering never ceased.
The evil truth of a mother and baby homes,
Kept hidden from the world.

The brave and innocent did endure.
Babies torn apart from their mother's arms.
Buried bodies scattered in septic tanks,
Shrouded bones longing for love and truth.

Religion held this vigil of neglect.
No tears shed at unmarked graves.
No prayers could justify their torment.
Innocent babies lost their lives.

With nobody to bless,
The Lost souls of Tuam.
With nobody to save,
The Lost souls of Tuam,
Corless released those lost babies
To their final resting place.
No longer buried to silent cries
Their story will never die.

*Kirsten Schaap*

# *BADB*

Linger dear Badb,
Between my palms, I will caress
You with the Celtic wilds.
My lips mutter deadly incantations, to
incite battles of Ireland's dreams.

Flying high with rebellious minds,
Fighting for freedom from savage sins.
I soar to shade wounded bodies,
Torn from battle from the heat.
They rise to the revolution
Fighting against the bloody doom.

A phantom among the dead,
Dear Badb.
Rise up.

*Liv Kristin Haakerud*

# WHITE FEATHERS

Let me tell you a story held in the wind,
A voice with no education, no freewill.
To speak for those who cannot reach,
Beyond the dirt beneath their feet.
I broke the silence screamed to the sky,
To highlight the torment of so many lives.
Innocent girls with white angel's wings,
Cut down and passed through evil rings.

Trafficked, used thrown aside,
Exploited, abused, wounded or killed.
Behind their eyes lived waves of dreams,
Crashing to the silence of their screams.
Salty tears filled ocean's wide
Emerging silhouettes, wings that cry.
I was washed up on the golden sands,
Rescued from their cruel demands.

I will tell you a story of a girl,
She had no name, no future life.
Under stormy skies she cried in rage,
To clear the horrors from her sight.
But when the storm is quiet and chilled,
She fights to help those tortured screams
We hear those voices in the wind,
Don't turn a blind eye to their dreams.
I am a girl with floating eyes,
White feathers keep me safe and alive.

*David Van Gough*

# UNCAGED DAYS

I'm cut from the earth, yet
Rooted to madness.
I'm straining to protect a world,
Caught inside graves of greed.

Vultures of wisdom, cry to our demise.
Lands forlorn, struggling in a world of fire,
Turn to darkness where everything dies.

A bird dropped some eyes, from
A fragile mind. They plant seeds into hands,
Creating thoughts for future lives.

The stronghold, the bark groans, strained.
A world encased travels through winds
Unravelling change into open minds.

Take my eyes to a higher plain.
Wash toxic tears from our lands.
Seasons burning in swift deliverance.
Shedding reasons into spiralling eyes.

I'm cut from the earth, bold and beautiful.
Fragile under a cracked sky,
Don't let me sleep to screeching vultures.
Uncaged days, we to need to survive.

*Biljana Milić*

# MASTER OF DREAMS

I travel in holy vessels, binding elements,
Repainting cruelty into kindness and truth.
Let me be the master of my own destiny,
Dancing in winds blowing against
Hypocrisy.
An easel coloured with nature's vision,
Seeks freedom of dreams in faraway lands.
A watchful sky yielding knowledge,
Absorbs all earthly things, an impartial eye.
I weep at humanity's self-destruction,
Through gales and blizzards,
Imposing chaos.
I travel through oceans' swirling depths,
Searching for truth and serenity.
I dream and dream against the gloom,
Crashing against tumultuous waves.
I am the universe of trembling light,
Travelling through time in burning suns.
I am the darkness in reverent soil,
Nourished by intellectual conscience.
I am the hand that holds you, in valleys
Shaded by hope.
Let me breathe in the natural balance,
Where dreams cut paths to hope.
I am the unseen river streaming thoughts
deep through your unconscious.
I am the winds of change
Breathing into your dreams.

*Kirsten Schaap*

# *HORIZONS UNEXPLORED*

The boundary between the fleshy
Human eye and the far seeing eagle's cry,
Holds the breath of decaying bodies.
Eyes watching immortality,
Flickering in candle light.
The unseen wrapped carefully in linen.

The boundaries between life and death
Expelled into infinite space.
Packed skin and bone, long turned to dust.
Searching for minds transcendent and wise.
Waiting for ascension to the stars.
Dissolved in mid-air, particles of those
Guiding hands, where nothing is denied.

Everything is invisible.
Light burning in empty spaces,
Creating a void where love resides.
In the cold-blooded eyes of the
King of the skies.

Transformation of the divine sparks
Aspirations. Waiting to observe, we fly
Beyond the vacuum of unexplored horizons.
Open your eyes wide.

# *MY BELOVED POETRY*

I want to get lost in the pages
As I roll back the edges,
Letting you climb in.
I trace the letters along your spine
Pausing to inhale your scent.
Breathing into the centre
Of affectionate rhymes.
Turning me back and forth,
Pages so engaging.
Wrapped around me.
We get lost in passages of the night,
Until the break of dawn.
I am an open book waiting to be read.
I am yours waiting to be explored,
I am a story waiting to happen.
I am the embodiment of love,
Waiting to be unlocked.

"The world of being; everything in this world "always is," "has no becoming," and "does not change"

It is apprehended by the understanding, not by the senses"

The world of becoming; everything in this world "comes to be and passes away, but never really is"

It is grasped by opinion and sense-perception.

The cosmos itself came into being, created using as its model the world of Forms."

-Plato

Printed in Poland
by Amazon Fulfillment
Poland Sp. z o.o., Wrocław

12113994R00047